LOVEDEN

Founder of Buscot Park

by

N. G. Shippobotham

LOVEDEN - Founder of Buscot Park

First published in the UK in 2015 by Stanford Publishing

ISBN 978-0-9560844-9-1

British Library Cataloguing in Publication Data. A catalogue record for this book is available from the British Library.

Typeset in Calibri, Candara and Mirror by 2m Partnership Limited
www.2m.org.uk

Printed and bound by Cambrian Printers

Stanford Publishing Limited
24 Chapel Road, Stanford in the Vale, Faringdon, Oxfordshire SN7 8LE, UK
Tel: +44(0)5600 737981 Email: enquiries@stanfordpublishing.co.uk
Website: www.stanfordpublishing.co.uk

Dedicated to

Jean Woof

1931 – 2010

Jean was a dear friend who
lived for many years at
Weston Farm, once part of
the Loveden estate.

JEC

~ PREFACE ~

This booklet was inspired by original research undertaken by J. E. Cradock BEd and is devoted to the life of Edward Loveden Loveden, the man responsible for the building of Buscot House and for the early development of its surrounding estate, known as Buscot Park.

Acknowledgements

In the course of our research we have been helped by many people. We are grateful to: The Bodleian Library, Oxford; The National Archives, Kew; Berkshire Record Office, Reading; and Faringdon Library, for access to their resources. Special thanks are owed to Mrs Janie Cottis for the use of her PhD thesis.

Thanks are due to the owners of copyrights for the use of the images in this booklet. We are particularly grateful to: Lord Faringdon and the Trustees of the Faringdon Collection for their permission to use copies of the painting of Buscot Park and of the miniature of Edward Loveden Loveden; to The Dean and Chapter of Christ Church, Oxford, for permission to show the photographs taken at Weston Farm; and to the Reverend David Williams of St Mary the Virgin, Buscot, for his permission to use photographs taken within the church and for his encouragement. The portrait of Edward Loveden is by permission of Llyfrgell Genedlaethol Cymru / The National Library of Wales.

The illustrative sketches in The Family chapter were specially commissioned from and donated by local artist Ruth Gerring.

We thank those friends who kindly read the proofs and offered their comments, and especially Roy Walker FRAgS for his advice and hospitality. However, we accept responsibility for any errors or omissions.

JEC, NGS March 2015

~ THE MAN ~

Edward Loveden Townsend was born in 1750 (see Notes), into a family whose maternal ancestors had been in possession of manorial land in Buscot since Elizabethan times, and he was educated at Winchester School and Trinity College, Oxford. The "manor of Buscot" was bequeathed to him by a great-uncle with the proviso that Edward must renounce the Townsend surname in favour of Loveden, which he did when he was twenty-one, so becoming Edward Loveden Loveden.

Edward Loveden Loveden, c. 1780
(National Library of Wales, G/E01 gcf02060)

He came into his inheritance at a time when the British Empire had expanded its territories on several continents and the Royal Navy had proved itself capable of defending the empire's interests. The early popularity and stability of Lord North's government, and the interest that George III took in agricultural improvements on his own estates (earning him the soubriquet 'farmer George'), may have fostered the spirit of enterprise that informed Edward's own future ambitions. However, it was to be seven years before he had the means to embark on the building of Buscot House and the surrounding park, including the 'model farm'.

Edward was prominent in public life and his interests were many: he was Sheriff of Berkshire in 1781 and of Brecon in 1799; he was a member of the Board of Agriculture from 1793 and Lieutenant Colonel of the Berkshire militia from 1794 to 1796; he was also Member of Parliament for Abingdon from 1783 to 1796 and for Shaftesbury in Dorset from 1802 to 1812. In addition, he became a Fellow of the Royal Society and of the Antiquarian Society.

Edward also played a significant role in the promotion of the Thames & Severn canal, which benefited the traffic through his lock on the Thames at Buscot Park, where he built the magnificent house and gardens that still stand at the heart of the estate.

Successful as he was in the public arena, his private life was overshadowed by sadness. Two marriages ended in the deaths of his wives at quite young ages and his third marriage led to protracted and distressing divorce proceedings. Three of the six children of his first marriage died young and a fourth was physically handicapped. Simply to repeat the cynical observation that Edward made "three provident marriages" is to discount these tragic circumstances.

Edward was a man of energy and purpose whether in matters of public duty or, as we shall see, in matters relating to the management of the Buscot estate. It has been suggested that Edward's determination to subjugate the river Thames to his will can, when viewed in conjunction with certain actions concerning his family, be read as evidence of a controlling nature. This may be a rather oversimplified judgement on what would have been seen in their time as 18th century norms.

Edward Loveden Loveden, 1795 by Richard Cosway RA

We might rather say of Edward that he acted in what he believed were the best interests of those concerned: in public matters he thought that what was good for the Buscot estate was good for his constituency and for the country; in private matters he thought that he had a moral duty to protect his own and his family's interests. Edward's good name was important to him and he felt entitled to maintain the honour of that name. If following his duty led him to be blind to some of his own defects of character – his temper, his high-handedness – at least he was not a cynical man.

Edward died in 1822 and an obituary of him acknowledged that "Few country gentlemen have performed a more honourable part in life than the deceased".

~ THE ESTATE ~

The parish of Buscot lies in the north-west corner of the Vale of White Horse, in what is now Oxfordshire but in Edward's time was in Berkshire. It is bounded by the river Cole in the west, separating it from Wiltshire (now Swindon), and by the river Thames in the north, whose opposite bank is in Gloucestershire.

Land and Buildings

The land use in the parish was determined by its topography and geology: the fields adjacent to the rivers Cole and Thames were ideal for the cultivation of grass and hence the grazing and dairying of cattle were the norm here; the higher ground, consisting of sedimentary rock, favoured arable farming further east in the county but was less suited to it in Buscot.

Land ownership in the mid-18th century parish of Buscot was vested in the Lovedens and other prominent families, such as the Throckmortons of Buckland, and in some Oxford colleges. The estate that was bequeathed to Edward by his great-uncle consisted of the "manor of Buscott and capital messuage called Weston House and closes thereto belonging", that is its surrounding homestead. However, when he came to build Buscot House, Edward chose a site that was not then within his estate: the land, on a local prominence in the east of the parish, was leased from the Throckmortons and the house replaced a barn called Farn Hill. From the elevated site there were views over the turnpike between Lechlade and Faringdon and across the grazing land along the banks of the Thames.

The map from Rocque's survey of Berkshire in 1761 shows: the village and church of Buscott; settlements at Buscott Wick and at Snowswick; the Barn (not then named as Farn Hill) and other named buildings at Weston and Mud House. There are unnamed buildings at sites corresponding to present-day Oldfield Farm, Pennyswick Farm and Broadleaze Farm.

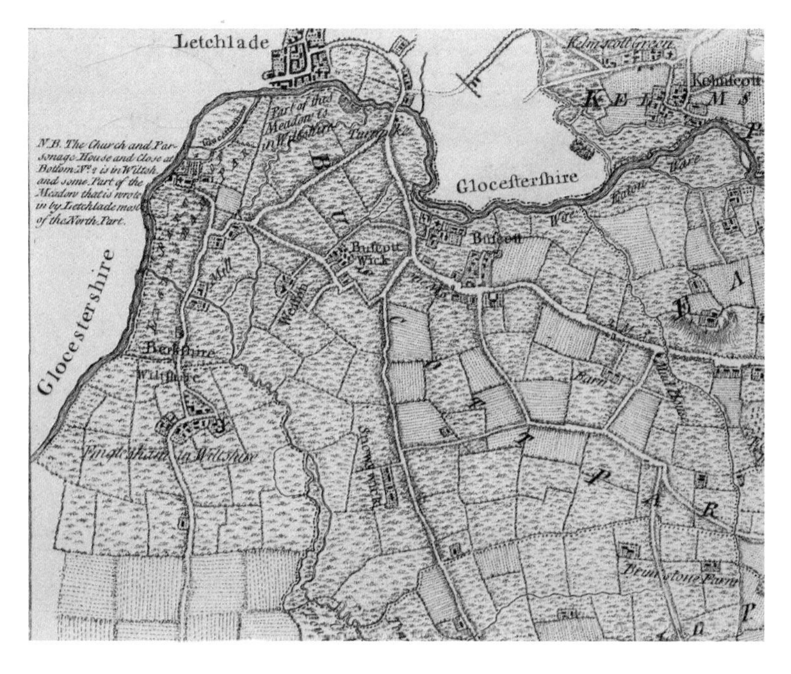

From J. Rocque's survey of Berkshire, 1761

The present building at Weston, now called Weston Farm, bears some plaques confirming that this became the home of the Lovedens from the middle of the 17th century. Buscot Manor, the manor house in Buscot village, dates from the William and Mary period and was the residence of a Loveden "lord of the manor" into the early part of the 18th century.

Buscot House

Although Edward may have had some influence over the design of the house, he employed "an able and experienced architect", James Darley, to carry out the building of both the house and the surrounding park, drawing on local labour and in large part local materials. The design was clearly influenced by Robert Adam, though the plan of the house was conventional rather than in the more classical Palladian style. The twin outer staircases led to the main door on the principal floor level and were both practical and still fashionable; a more elaborate example can be seen at Kedleston Hall in Derbyshire, designed by Adam in 1761.

The Park

By 1782 the majority of the work on the new house was complete and attention could be turned to the parkland. In that year paling was completed and deer were introduced, underground drainage begun, the fishpond dug and trees planted. The park was then sown with grass in the following spring. At this time the grounds consisted of "120 acres of parkland pasture, 5 acres of water, 23 acres of plantation and 5 acres of kitchen garden, plus one acre of shrubbery around the house".

The size of the stable block, as well the attention paid to its architectural detail, was in keeping with the stature of the main house and reflected the importance of horses to a gentleman's household. Edward's account books refer to the stabling of horses in many towns, locally and as far afield as Bath, Bristol and London, for both practical and leisure purposes. It is clear, too, that game shooting and fishing were country pursuits with which Edward would have entertained parties of friends and guests.

There were also accounts for the kitchen garden, which was larger than usual for a house the size of Buscot Park. Edward himself kept a record of more than 300 fruit trees that were planted, with notes on their variety, taste and so on. Set to the east side of the main house, an orangery was built in about 1790 and would have housed 'fine plants' acquired in Bath and London. There was a vogue for such pastimes but it was typical of Edward that his interest was not superficial; in time he would become a Fellow of the Horticultural Society of London, now the Royal Horticultural Society.

Expansion

Partly through his wives' inheritances, partly with the help of mortgages and partly due to the efficient management of the estate, Edward was able to spend considerable sums to increase his ownership of land, both in Buscot and in the surrounding parishes. Thus it was that in 1788 he finally acquired from the Throckmortons the land on which Buscot House stood and within ten years he owned much of the land in his home parish. He further developed the estate by introducing a twenty-acre lake, extending the deer park and incorporating more heathland and pasture into the park.

~ THE FARM ~

In his 1724 work, 'A Tour Through the Whole Island of Great Britain', Daniel Defoe said of Berkshire:

"If the soil is not everywhere naturally fertile yet cultivation supplies all its defects and produces a large increase. The most fruitful tracts lie on the banks of the rivers Thames and Kennet and in the Vale of White Horse. Wheat and every other species of corn are the staple commodities of the inhabitants, of which by the conveyance of the river Thames they send amazing quantities to the London market weekly; and the barley and malt are excellent."

Thus the farm at Buscot was blessed in its location and we can suppose that Edward's Loveden ancestors were among those landowners able to send "amazing quantities" of produce to London.

The enclosure of common land at Buscot had occurred more than a century earlier than Defoe's tour but it was during the period between 1770 and 1810 that most of the parishes in the Vale of White Horse followed suit. Once land had been enclosed it became possible for individual owners to make their own improvements and the old open field system disappeared to be replaced by the patchwork of hedged fields that we appreciated until only recently.

Meanwhile, a remarkably influential work, 'The Horse Hoeing Husbandry', by the Berkshire agriculturalist Jethro Tull, was to generate considerable controversy and opposition when it was published in 1731. It advocated a more systematic approach to sowing seed by the use of drills and hoeing implements, as opposed to the old scattering of seeds. In this country it would be a hundred years before Tull's system met with general acceptance.

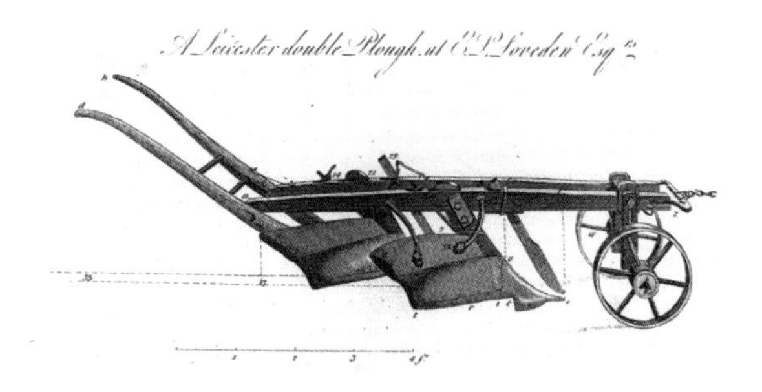

A Leicester double Plough at E. L. Loveden Esqrs.

Surprisingly, the book found early favour in France and developments made there had filtered back to these islands by 1760, eventually taking root in the minds of a later generation of Berkshire farmers.

By the time that William Mavor had compiled his exhaustive report, a 'General View of the Agriculture of Berkshire', in 1809, Edward was using implements at Buscot that had been inspired by and had evolved from Tull's ideas.

Mavor reports, "The farming establishment at Buscot Park, which is eligibly situated on rather a level spot, at a suitable distance from the mansion house, is replete with every accommodation; and might serve as a model for a farm of such magnitude... in farms utility alone should be consulted, and it should always be combined with economy".

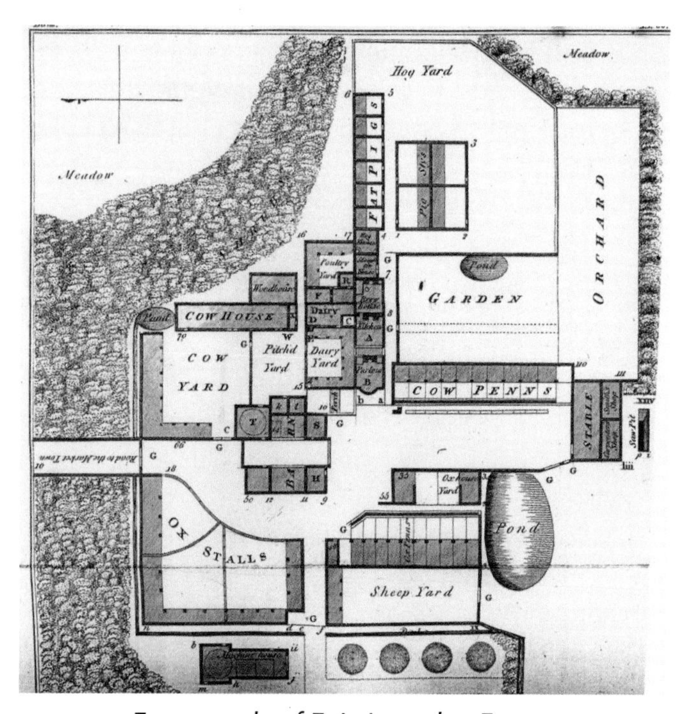

Farm-yards of E. L. Loveden Esqr.
"A model for a farm"

Edward had probably made piecemeal additions to the farm layout as new ideas came to him, because, as Mavor notes, "that excellently as Mr Loveden's farm appendages are adapted to the various purposes for which they were intended, had they been built at once, and from an uniform plan, it is probable that the parts would have been less broken and intermixed".

Edward experimented with the drainage and irrigation of his fields beside the Thames in efforts to increase their productivity; he found that he could mow grass to make hay earlier in the year and claimed that this hay increased the milk yield of the cows that fed on it.

Through the activities of the Berkshire Agricultural Society, of which Edward was a co-founder in the early 1790s, farmers were able to exchange information about new methods and their experiences of using them – though the society did suffer internal divisions along political lines that led to its demise, before resurfacing in 1800. It also ran competitions that we would recognize in modern agricultural shows.

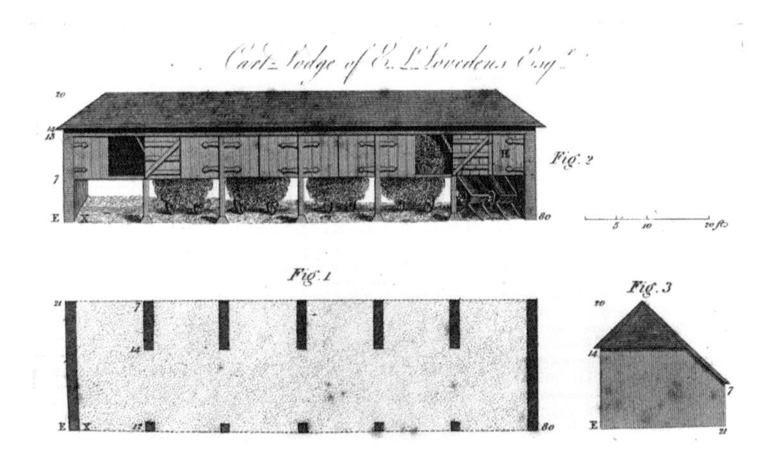

Cart Lodge of E. L. Loveden Esqr.

Among many breeds of sheep, Berkshires and Southdowns were considered the best adapted and hardiest types for the dry soils and downs in the county but some farmers, including Edward, preferred the merits of Leicesters and Coteswolds, of which he had a fine flock at Buscot. In a typical year his flock might yield more than three hundred fleeces for an income of around £100 (see Notes). Sheep markets and wool fairs became a feature of the area.

Dairying was practised in many localities in Berkshire and butter was made for sale in Oxford and London as well as for local use. Buscot became one of the principal centres for the transport of cheese. Edward had a small wharf built beside the Thames at Buscot, with warehouses for the storage of cheese, and these were rented by London cheesemongers. About one thousand tons of cheese were sent down the Thames each year from Berkshire alone, representing between one third and one half of all the cheese sent by that route.

Drip stone from a cheese press

Mavor says that Edward's dairy was "very complete. To his cheese presses and churn he has applied Garnett's patent inventions, which diminish labour, and are found to be attended with every advantage that can be expected from them." It was that same diminishment of labour, which the new implements enabled, that had roused the early opposition of agricultural labourers to the innovations sparked by Tull's system, in much the same way that the mechanisation of tasks associated with the textile industry would lead to the actions of the Luddites.

The cheese of those days was similar to present-day single Gloucester (and it's worth remarking that only a handful of producers of single Gloucester cheese remain today). Snowswick Farm, bought by Edward in 1806, made their cheeses in the shape of pineapples and these had "a peculiar richness and delicacy of flavour", while at Stanford in the Vale and Goosey they came in the shape of a sitting hare.

Edward once bought a very fine breeding bull for forty-five guineas, but he generally bred cattle from within Buscot's own Hereford stock and sometimes bought in Scottish heifers to be either fattened up for sale or retained for milk.

Mr. Loveden's Hereford Bull
"A model of symmetry and completeness"

The farm also kept pigs and the Berkshires he specialised in were renowned at home and abroad as a breeding stock. An example of the ingenious and efficient design of Edward's farm is the arrangement by which skimmed milk was allowed to flow directly from the dairy into the troughs at which the pigs fed.

Mr. Loveden's Berkshire Hog

As well as skimmed milk the pigs were fed with boiled potatoes, barley, beans and pulses. Mavor tells us that "The greatest part of the pigs slaughtered in Berkshire are made into bacon. About four thousand are killed at Faringdon alone between Michaelmas and April. They are cured in the usual way and dried, in proper store rooms, with wood or coal." But it seems to have been the skimmed milk that made the difference because, without the dairying connection, commercial pig-keeping was regarded as unprofitable beyond the use of the manure for fertilizer.

Even the orchards benefited from Edward's inventive mind: he had canvas awnings made to protect the fruit from frost and blight.

The grounds of Buscot Park already included a fish-pond but Edward erected a purpose-built "fish house that cannot be robbed" close by the banks of the Thames, next to his lock. It was made secure so that even the lock-keeper, whose home it was, could not access the fish that were trapped beneath it.

Footnote

The site of Edward's model farm has not yet been established but may have been in the vicinity of Buscot Manor, the late 17th century Loveden residence and itself later used as a farmhouse. There are 18th/19th century farm buildings nearby, one of which bears a resemblance to the cart lodge illustrated earlier, but no evidence that they belonged to the original model farm.

It is sad to relate that after Edward's death and in the years leading up to the eventual sale of the Buscot Park estate in 1859 his model farm had "fallen into entire neglect". Fortunately, the estate was to be saved by a new owner, Robert Tertius Campbell, who seems to have incarnated the spirit of Edward Loveden Loveden in the energy and inventiveness that he applied to the redevelopment of Buscot Park.

~ THE CANAL ~

It had long been the dream of traders and travellers to improve communication between the commercial and population centres of Bristol and London. Road transport was slow and could be hazardous; in winter it was often impossible. Hence many schemes were put forward as early as the seventeenth century to link the two cities by making a canal that would connect the navigable stretches of the rivers Severn and Thames.

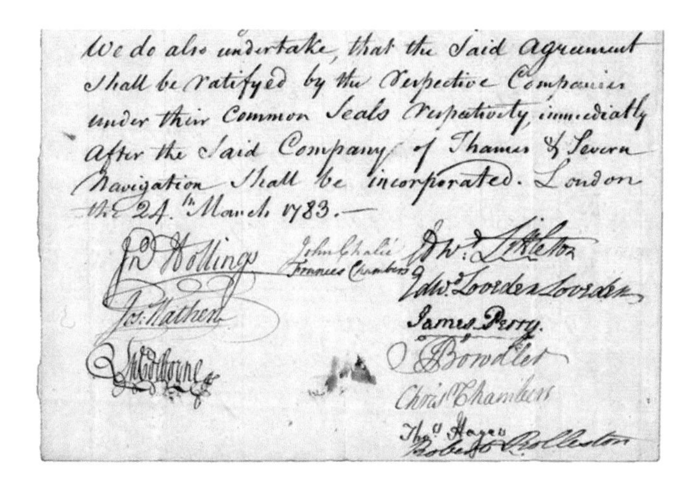

We do also undertake, that the said agreement shall be ratifyed by the respective Companies under their Common Seals respectively, immediatly after the said Company of Thames & Severn Navigation shall be incorporated. London the 24.th March 1783.—

James Perry.

Signatures of the Thames and Severn Proprietors, 1783 (Gloucestershire Archives GRO D1180/4/43)

As the owner of a private lock on the Thames at Buscot, Edward would have had a clear financial interest in such a canal, which would enable the through-passage of goods and people to and from the West Country. Even without a canal, five thousand tons of cargo were being shipped annually from Lechlade through Buscot Lock to London and these included industrial metals and nails, as well as the cheese from Edward's wharf. In the other direction came coal from Newcastle, timber, farm produce and other goods.

So it is no surprise that Edward became a promoter of and shareholder in The Company of Proprietors of the Thames and Severn Canal Navigation in 1781. It took two years for the company to get the consent of a parliamentary act for the building and operation of a canal that would join the eastern end of the already operational Stroudwater Navigation to the Thames at Inglesham, just above Lechlade.

The canal was six years in construction and its main line was just less than 29 miles long; it was 12 feet wide and the draft was five feet; it had 44 locks and connecting to the Stroudwater Navigation involved the building of the Sapperton Tunnel – at that time the longest canal tunnel in England at 3817 yards.

The first boat passed through the Inglesham Lock on 19th November 1789, to the cheers of an assembled crowd and the booming of a twelve-cannon salute from Buscot Park. Even so, there remained concerns among the shareholders regarding the state of the river downstream from Buscot.

The Thames Commissioners administered the river between Lechlade and Abingdon and were responsible for maintaining its navigability. This body was run by a committee of fifteen of its most active members – including Edward – and personal interests frequently influenced their judgements. Despite Edward's strong support of the use of modern lock designs, the Commissioners were ineffective in bringing about sufficient improvements on the river above Abingdon.

This lack of progress resulted in the House of Commons setting up a committee of enquiry in 1793, to be chaired by Edward, who, as the MP for Abingdon, could not have been regarded as the most impartial choice. Despite the enquiry's condemnation of the Commissioners' failings, the essential measures for which Edward argued to bring improvements to the upper Thames were not acted on by parliament.

As for its shareholders, the Thames and Severn Canal was never able to generate the anticipated return on their capital. For one thing, the cost of constructing it was nearly double the initial capitalisation of the company. For another, its financial management was lax and the company found itself with large debts. Finally, the effects of leakages and the difficulty of maintaining an adequate supply of water had been underestimated and, in spite of erecting a pump to bring groundwater to the rescue, these problems were not overcome. Such setbacks, combined with the unimproved state of the Thames above Abingdon, meant that the imagined east-west commerce would never reach levels that might have rendered the canal company profitable. In the end, the real beneficiaries of the canal were the communities through which it passed and the merchants and proprietors (including Edward, of course) whose business it carried.

Edward also fought rearguard actions in opposing the Wiltshire & Berkshire Canal, which would bypass Buscot Lock and which was eventually completed in 1810. He

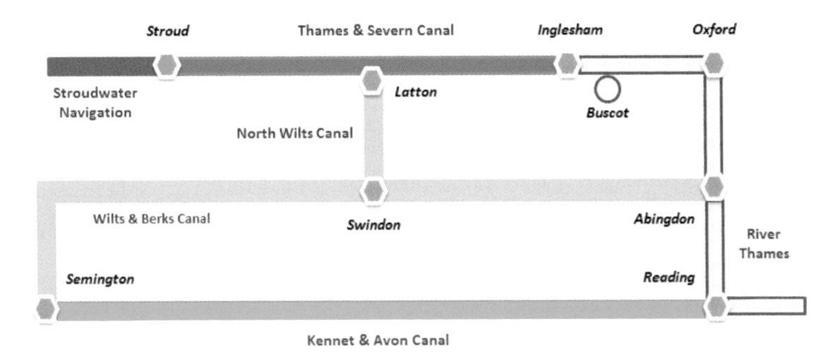

Canals associated with the River Thames

resigned from the company in 1812 but persisted in his objections, as a proprietor, and famously lost his temper when a decision went against him on the North Wiltshire Canal, which opened in 1819.

Nevertheless, the involvement of Edward over so many years in efforts to improve and protect the Thames, and by doing so to secure the traffic through his lock at Buscot, led William Mavor to comment: "So much was he attached to the prince of British streams, on whose banks a large portion of his estate lay, that he used to be called, jocularly by his friends, 'Old Father Thames,' an application which he did not dislike on suitable occasions".

~ THE FAMILY ~

Edward Loveden Loveden left no diaries that we know of; he wrote no autobiography; among the Loveden Papers there are very few of his own private letters. In the absence of personal reminiscences, what can we say about his family life, the life beyond the public face?

We can present the facts of his marriages and of his case for divorce; we can name his children and his grandchildren; we can gaze on his likeness. We can read his will but can we read his character?

Plaques at Weston Farm house

There were Lovedens occupying the manor of Buscot for a hundred years before Roger Loveden and his wife Alice lived at what is now Weston Farm, close to Buscot Wick, in the 17th century (see Loveden Family Tree 1). Carved stone plaques, one with the initials L-R-A and the date 1659 and the other with the Loveden arms (sideways), can still be seen in a wall of the farmhouse.

A new house was built in Buscot village in about 1691 and this became the residence of Roger and Alice's grandson

Captain John Loveden, who was known as "lord of Buscot manor" and died unmarried in 1741. Thus the manor passed to John's brother Edward, the last surviving male of the Loveden line. It was the desire of this remaining Loveden, who styled himself 'of Weston House' and who died unmarried in 1749, that his land and properties should be bequeathed to a Loveden; he therefore made it a condition of his will that the eventual beneficiary must change their surname to Loveden before they could inherit. So it was that his estate was left to the first male heir of his niece Jane Townsend who attained the age of twenty-one and this heir was not born until a year after his great-uncle's death.

—

Some doubt persists as to the exact date of Edward's birth or baptism but one source suggests that he was born Edward Loveden Townsend on Thursday, 11th October, 1750 at Cirencester in the county of Gloucester. He was the son of Thomas Townsend, a gentleman, and his wife Jane Baker, whose own mother had been a Loveden from Buscot. The Townsends had property in Bisley, Gloucestershire.

At the beginning of 1756 the Townsends buried two children at Buscot, but it is not certain that the family had relocated there yet. It was when Edward was five years old that these two younger brothers died; then when he was six his mother died, leaving his father with three youngsters to bring up, namely Edward, his sister Jane and another baby brother, Robert Baker. Such losses, and at such a tender age, doubtless coloured the upbringing of the young boy.

Edward attended Winchester School between the ages of about 11 and 14 but in January 1767, when he was 16, his father died and for Edward that must have signalled the end of his childhood and the beginning of his adult life. Because Edward was destined to inherit his great-uncle's Loveden estate, his father passed almost the whole of the Townsend estate to Edward's sister Jane, leaving Edward just a "plate which came from Merton". At the time of their father's death the three orphaned childen were all under the age of twenty-one and were left in the care of a guardian, Richard Butler of Painswick.

A few months later in the same year, and still only 16 years old, Edward was admitted to Trinity College, Oxford, as a Gentleman-Commoner, a rank of student above commoners but below noblemen, enjoying special privileges but having to pay higher fees. He seems to have been a handsome young man; he acquired a love of classical literature and was well read, as the eventual extent of his library attested.

By this time it was clear that Edward was to be the ultimate beneficiary of his great-uncle's will and that he would have to comply with the proviso that he should renounce his paternal surname Townsend and substitute the name of Loveden. On reaching his majority, he applied for a royal licence to effect the change and it was granted the day before his 22nd birthday in 1772. Henceforth he would be known as Edward Loveden Loveden, Esquire, of Buscot and we can reasonably presume that he (and perhaps his siblings) would now have occupied Weston House, the home of the great-uncle from whom he inherited, though it is possible they might have chosen the manor house in Buscot village.

Edward's schooling and elevation to the gentry could not entirely erase the shades of his upbringing, however. A fellow parliamentarian many years later wrote of him, "His figure, manners, and dress all bespoke a substantial yeoman rather than a person of education and condition; but he did not want plain common sense, nor language in which to clothe his ideas".

—

To quote another, rather better known author: "It is a truth universally acknowledged, that a single man in possession of a good fortune, must be in want of a wife." Edward was no exception to this rule.

His first marriage, in 1773 at the age of 22, was to Margaret (see Loveden Family Tree 2), the sole heiress of Lewis Pryse, who had interests at Woodstock in Oxfordshire and Gogerddan in Cardiganshire and whose ancestors claimed descent from Edward I. A son and two daughters were soon followed by a second son and one can imagine that domestic life at the family home was happy and comfortable and centred on the needs of the four young children. But a month after the birth of the new son both the baby, Walter Pryse, and the younger daughter, Jane Grace, had died and they were buried together on the same day in Buscot Church in 1777.

Two years passed and another son, Edward, was born but he died within a day or two of his baptism. It was in this same sad year of 1779 that Margaret's father died and she inherited his estate. In the face of these reminders of their own mortality, Edward and Margaret affirmed their faith in God by making generous gifts to Buscot Church. Perhaps, too, in an effort to put the tragedies of the recent years behind them, Edward embarked on the building of a new home for the family, a home that would be commensurate with their wealth and standing.

For the next two years Edward would doubtless have been involved with the plans for the new house and have made frequent visits to witness the construction. And this would have been in addition to the normal pursuits and responsibilities of a gentleman of his means. The new mansion was being built little more than a mile by the turnpike road from Buscot; it was on a hill and at a healthy distance from the damp, Thames air that must have lingered around the village.

In 1781 Edward felt that he could afford the time to devote himself to the office of High Sheriff of Berkshire, though he appears only to have served for seven months or so. By October of that year the building was being roofed: did Edward take his young family - the boy, Pryse, now seven years old and his sister, Margaret, six – to see their new home as it neared completion a year later? Did they stand atop the double staircase on the south front and survey the land that had been cleared and was being laid as parkland?

In the spring of 1783 Edward was elected to parliament for the constituency of Abingdon, just a month before

the family was blessed with the arrival of another girl, Jane Elizabeth. The house and the parkland – to be known together as Buscot Park – were now complete and doubtless the family will have moved into their magnificent new home before the winter set in.

Jane Elizabeth was baptised at Buscot Church on 24th June 1783; we don't know if she was handicapped from birth but she was to spend most of her life in a wheelchair. Her birth was attended by one of the most remarkable meteorological events in Britain's history.

The Hampshire naturalist Gilbert White would note:

"By my journal I find that I had noticed this strange occurrence from June 23 to July 20 inclusive, during which period the wind varied to every quarter without making any alteration in the air. The sun, at noon, looked as blank as

a clouded moon, and shed a rust-coloured ferruginous light on the ground, and floors of rooms; but was particularly lurid and blood-coloured at rising and setting. All the time the heat was so intense that butchers' meat could hardly be eaten on the day after it was killed; and the flies swarmed so in the lanes and hedges that they rendered the horses half frantic, and riding irksome. The country people began to look, with a superstitious awe, at the red, louring aspect of the sun."

Earlier in June a volcano had erupted in Iceland and it spewed out a sulphurous haze for the next eight months. Many thousands of people in Britain died and outdoor workers were especially affected. Hot weather caused severe thunderstorms throughout the summer and into autumn, accompanied by large hailstones that were reported to have killed cattle. The following winter was extremely severe and White recorded 28 days of continuous frost.

It was towards the end of this harsh and unprecedented winter – and possibly because of it – that Margaret herself died in February 1784 at the tragically early age of 36. Edward, bereft and with three young and now motherless children, placed a memorial plaque in the parish church at Buscot that speaks movingly of his beloved wife.

In the following year Edward, not yet 35 years old, married Mrs Elizabeth Nash, the widow of Joseph Nash, a wealthy hop merchant, and the sole heiress of her father John Darker, of Gayton in Northamptonshire. Elizabeth had at least two children from her first marriage and it is possible that her daughter (Mary?) lived with her at Buscot Park. There were no children of this second

marriage and Elizabeth, too, was fated to die young, at the age of 34 in February 1788. Again, the memorial plaque in the parish church stands as a testament to Edward's love and loss. (Both memorials appear in the chapter on The Parish & The Church.)

During the brief years of his marriage to Elizabeth, Edward had continued as MP for Abingdon. Nominally a Whig (see Notes), he held his own opinions and was frequently at odds with his fellow Whig MPs and his constituents. Despite this he was returned unchallenged in the 1790 election. However, the events in France, which led to its being declared a republic in 1792, saw Edward return to the government fold in an uncharacteristic show of solidarity.

The deaths of Edward's two wives had brought increases to his annual income of £1,000 and £4,500 respectively, which, in addition to the legacy from his great-uncle, gave him a total income of more than £8,000 a year. At forty years of age he could count himself a very wealthy gentleman. However, he had also incurred debts of above £50,000 in building Buscot House and in enlarging the estate with further acquisitions of land.

We may suppose that the older children had by now had some sort of education. We do know that Edward's son, Pryse Loveden, was sent to Eton and then went up to Christ Church College, Oxford, in 1792, when he was about 18.

The year 1793 saw Edward increasingly involved in public affairs: he was the co-founder of the Board of Agriculture (the forerunner of the Ministry of Agriculture, Fisheries and Food – now DEFRA); and he presided over a parliamentary committee on Thames navigation. All this was in addition to his normal constituency business and to overseeing the management of his estate. In recognition of his work, he was awarded the degree of Doctor of Laws by Oxford University; this was often an honorary award to someone active in public life, usually in the field of politics or the law. It may be argued that his public concerns were related directly to matters on which the continued prosperity of his estate might depend, but perhaps he judged that what was good for his estate was good for his constituents.

—

In 1794 Edward contracted his third marriage, to Anne Lintall (or Lenthall), the daughter of a Northampton squire; Edward was now in his early forties and Anne was half his age. At this time, Edward was pursuing his interests in the fields of politics, agricultural development and canals – from which the wealth of his estate flowed – and simultaneously held high rank in the Berkshire militia. His devotion to these many duties led to frequent absences from his household and the long term consequence was that his marriage to Anne suffered.

Perhaps the loss of a child, stillborn, early in the marriage, which left Anne unable to have children, contributed to a lack of involvement in the life at Buscot Park and left her with time weighing heavily on her hands. The elder children of Edward's first marriage were only a year or two younger than Anne and one imagines that their relationship with Anne cannot have been easy. The youngest child Jane Elizabeth was about 11 years old when she was introduced to her second stepmother. Being disabled, Jane Elizabeth spent her days confined to a wheelchair in the rooms on the ground floor.

Lack of involvement was something that Edward could never be accused of: when he wasn't away from the house attending to his many interests, he was playing host to visitors and friends. In 1795 a belated twenty-first birthday party for his son was celebrated when "a most elegant ball and supper was given at Buscot Park" for Captain Pryse Loveden, only one of many parties that were enjoyed at the house during this period.

In that same year of 1795, Edward's only surviving sibling, his sister Jane Townsend, married the Rector of Tidmarsh and went to live in his parish near Reading. In the General Election of 1796 Edward stood as one of two Whig candidates for Berkshire but came third in the poll behind the Tory.

In the January of 1798 Pryse Loveden's grandmother, Margaret Pryse, died; she had been a widow for nearly nineteen years. Margaret's will nominated Pryse Loveden as her sole executor and major beneficiary. In February Pryse Loveden married the Honourable Harriet Agar, a widow and a daughter of the 2nd Viscount Ashbrook. By the time that his grandmother's will had been proved, in May, Pryse had changed his surname by royal licence, becoming Pryse Pryse (although unlike his father this renaming had not been a condition of his inheritance). Pryse would now have moved out of his childhood home Buscot Park and started his married life at his late grandmother's house at Woodstock, near Oxford.

—

As far as we know, life at Buscot Park will have continued with the usual round of social, business and recreational engagements for Edward, while Anne's only companion now was Edward's daughter Jane Elizabeth, ten years younger and attended by a female servant who looked after her needs in the wheelchair. They would spend eight or nine months of the year at Buscot Park and the rest at a rented house in London.

Edward, no longer a Member of Parliament, was in 1799 appointed the High Sheriff of Breconshire, in which county he owned land at Llangorse and other localities. In 1802 he stood again for a seat in the House and was elected MP for Shaftesbury in Dorset, a constituency he was to serve for the next ten years.

It was in 1804 that there began the fateful course of events that would end in public embarrassment for Edward and his wife. Some years earlier, Edward had assisted the son of a close friend when he went up to Oxford. The Barkers resided at Fairford Park, a large estate in Gloucestershire about 8 miles from Buscot, and Thomas Raymond Barker was a younger son of the family. Thomas had been made a Fellow of Merton in 1802 and it was his habit to call in at

Buscot Park on his journeys to and from Oxford. On some of these occasions Edward would have been absent and Thomas would have been the guest of Anne. Anne was in her early thirties and Thomas some six years younger.

By 1805 the relationship between Thomas and Anne – coyly termed "partiality" at the outset – had been noticed by servants in the Buscot Park household. As if foreshadowing a Jane Austen plot, it progressed to walking arm in arm, to exchanges of letters and to rumours of intimacy. The couple grew more incautious and one day Edward found them together in Anne's dressing room. He was minded to send Anne back to her mother but he sought counsel from a friend, who advised him that there was no evidence of serious misconduct and that Barker flirted with "every woman he came near". The friend also warned Thomas that Edward had his suspicions and there the matter lay – for a while.

Anne's father had died in 1799 and perhaps the lack of parental influence was a contributing factor in her reckless behaviour; her mother came to visit Buscot Park in 1807 and stayed for a year but, since Anne found her mother a bore, this had little effect in curbing her desire for Thomas's company. Instead Anne arranged to spend two nights at Fairford Park, expressly against Edward's wishes. Once again, Edward was persuaded that his belief in his wife's innocence had not been betrayed.

The months spent in London did nothing to dampen the couple's ardour; Thomas turned up in London and Anne would go out in her carriage and collect him. Back again at Buscot Park in 1808, Anne concocted a scheme to enable Thomas to sneak into the house after dark on a night

when Edward was away but her arrangements made the servants suspicious and they kept watch. Thomas was caught and appealed to the butler Warren Hastings not to inform Edward; he swore on his word of honour that he would not visit the house again. Likewise Anne promised not to communicate with or see Thomas again. The butler relented, probably hoping to protect the good name of his master.

It was no use. The couple continued to correspond and Anne made yet another attempt to smuggle Thomas into the house; again the servants were on to it. This time the butler remained implacable and sent word to Edward, who was staying with his son at Woodstock, exposing the whole affair. Edward is said to have burst into tears when faced with the evidence and straight away he sent Pryse to Buscot Park to order Anne out of the family home, which he did in the presence of his sister Jane Elizabeth. It was March 1809.

Edward set in motion proceedings to bring about a divorce and these came to court in 1810: he sued Thomas Raymond Barker for 'criminal conversation' (adultery), claiming £10,000 in damages, but Thomas was acquitted; he sued Anne for her adultery and he succeeded; Anne appealed but withdrew her appeal at the last moment;

Edward then sought a bill in parliament for divorce on the grounds of Anne's adultery and the bill passed through the Lords but was amended by the House of Commons to allow Anne alimony of £400 a year; Edward was furious at this apparent leniency towards Anne and so he withdrew the bill. Thus the divorce was not in fact completed.

This whole process took more than a year and all three parties lost by it: Thomas resigned his Fellowship at Merton with his reputation in ruins; Anne was exiled from the family home yet was still bound in marriage; and Edward was the innocent but betrayed husband who had been saved by his servants' vigilance and was returning to a home without a wife for a companion.

There was another, overlooked family member who also suffered a loss during this period. Jane Elizabeth, Edward's chairbound daughter, was 25 years old when Anne was sent away. It appears that she had received in that same year of 1809 a proposal of marriage from a Mr R. Weeks, a protégé of Edward's. When Edward learnt of this he summarily dismissed Mr Weeks from Buscot

Park. Thus the promise of a life of happiness was snuffed out; Jane Elizabeth would never marry.

After the separation and the abandonment of the divorce proceedings, the only Loveden family members left at Buscot Park were Edward and Jane Elizabeth. Around them were the familiar servants, including those that had tried to shield Edward from knowledge of Anne's indiscretions. The trial records mention Edward's butler Warren Hastings and the housekeeper, Hannah Calcott (probably the same Hannah Calcott who had been a servant for Margaret Pryse at Woodstock); also mentioned are a cook, an under-keeper, a footman, Robert Major an under-butler and Thomas Hooper a manservant. Jane Elizabeth's attendant was named as Anne Strange and Anne's personal maid had been Elizabeth Haynes. The aftermath of Edward's separation must have weighed heavily on the whole household.

The final decade of Edward's life saw his resignation from the Thames & Severn canal company in 1812; he then gave up his seat as MP for Shaftesbury the following year. This does not mean that Edward lost interest in life. Already in 1805 he had been elected a Fellow of the Royal Society and he was a Fellow of the Society of Antiquaries, so at the age of sixty he may have chosen to give precedence to his intellectual interests over his public affairs. It may also be that after the exposure resulting from the divorce proceedings he found private pursuits more congenial.

We have referred to Edward as the "innocent but betrayed husband" and nowhere have we questioned that innocence. Yet there is evidence of another side to his life. Harriet Thayer was born in about 1791, between Edward's second and third marriages; her antecedents are as yet unidentified (though she may have been related to the Townsend branch of the family). In September 1808 – before Anne's affair with Thomas Barker was made known – Edward drafted "instructions for my will" and by this will he intended "to settle upon Harriet Thayer, my daughter, now living with F[rancis] Knight, seven thousand pounds for her own use and benefit". It is possible that she was Edward's ward but it looks as if she was his natural (that is illegitimate) daughter. Harriet was known to other members of the family and there is at least one letter in which Edward's son Pryse addresses her as "my dear sister".

Whatever Harriet's status, she is mentioned a dozen times in Edward's final will (1818) and its three codicils (1821): she is left an annuity of £400; he leaves her his shares in three canals and his turnpike securities; she receives the contents of any house that he occupies (excluding Buscot House); and a pew in the chapel in Albermarle Street (probably St George's Chapel in Mayfair); and lastly he left Harriet his share in the British Institution in Pall Mall, an art gallery for connoisseurs – Harriet's portrait had been painted by the artist Thomas Lawrence and shown at the Royal Academy in about 1813.

Edward died at Buscot Park on 4th January 1822 at the age of 71. His will was proved on 30th May that year and Buscot Park and his other estates and interests, which must have been worth in total tens of thousands of pounds, passed to his son Pryse. Edward's butler Warren Hastings, who had once taken upon himself the responsibility of protecting Edward's reputation, received for his years of loyal and devoted service the sum of fifty pounds.

—

Edward's last will and testament disposes of those parts of his legacy that are measurable in acres and pounds sterling, and of his goods and chattels. But what of his human legacy – his surviving family?

His son Pryse Pryse had already inherited the 30,000-acre Cardiganshire estate of Gogerddan from his grandmother and now he was the master of Buscot Park. His first marriage had ended in tragedy after fifteen childless years, when his wife Harriet burnt to death in a fire during New Year celebrations at Gogerddan in 1813. Pryse shut himself away and for two years was looked after by a maid, Jane Cavallier.

Pryse married Jane when she fell pregnant and they soon had three children, who were baptised privately. After he inherited Buscot Park, his children were re-baptised at Buscot church, all on the same day in 1823. Pryse went on to serve twice as MP for Cardigan between 1818 and his death in 1849. His grandson sold the 3,500-acre Buscot estate in 1859.

In 1796 and against her father's wishes, Edward's elder daughter Margaret married Samuel Wilson Warneford, from the landed family at Sevenhampton near Highworth in Wiltshire. Samuel was an ordained priest as well as a man of property in his own right. He used his own wealth, together with money that Margaret had inherited from her Pryse grandfather, to undertake philanthropic enterprises (including what is known today as the Warneford Hospital in Oxford). Margaret died in 1840 and Samuel in 1855, aged 91, in the rectory at Bourton on the Hill, Gloucestershire.

Loveden House, Aberystwyth

Next we come to Edward's younger daughter Jane Elizabeth Loveden. Jane went to live at her brother's estate of Gogerddan, near Aberystwyth, and resided for a time in the family's town house, built by her brother and known as Loveden House, in Bridge Street, Aberystwyth. The story is that she travelled about in an adapted wheelchair that was pulled by a donkey and on Sundays she would be carried in a sedan chair to attend church.

There is a memorial to her in the church at Llanbadarn Fawr, near Aberystwyth, that reads:

"To the memory of Jane Elizabeth Loveden, youngest daughter of Edward Loveden Loveden, Esqr., of Buscot Park in the county of Berks, by his first wife, Miss Pryse of Gogerddan in this county. She died at Penybont, July 15th 1855, in her 72nd year, and is buried in the family vault in this Church. She is now before her judge. This tablet was erected by her nephews and niece as a small tribute to the memory of her many virtues."

Edward's wife Anne Loveden had been exiled from the marital home for thirteen years. She and Thomas Barker had moved away and settled together in Hambleden, a village in Buckinghamshire. Anne's death in 1821 meant that she did not outlive Edward and thus the couple were never able to marry. Thomas was the principal beneficiary of Anne's will and he was also provided for in his father's will of 1827. Thomas did eventually marry and he died in 1866 at the age of 88.

Finally we come to Harriet Thayer. Not long after Edward's death she married a French army instructor and amateur antiquarian, Adolphe Thiebault, and the following year they had a daughter Henrietta Malvina. The family travelled a lot and these journeys are recorded in a biography by Adolphe of their life together and in illustrations done by him of the places in which they stayed in England and France. Their marriage lasted thirty-eight years and Harriet's letters testify to a contented family life. In 1852 their daughter married and subsequently had children of her own. Harriet died in 1860.

The entry for Buscot ('Boroardescote') in the Domesday Book of 1086 shows that the village then had a relatively large population of 27 villagers, 31 smallholders and 6 slaves. Its resources included 300 acres of meadow and one fishery, as well as about 2400 acres of arable land (see Notes).

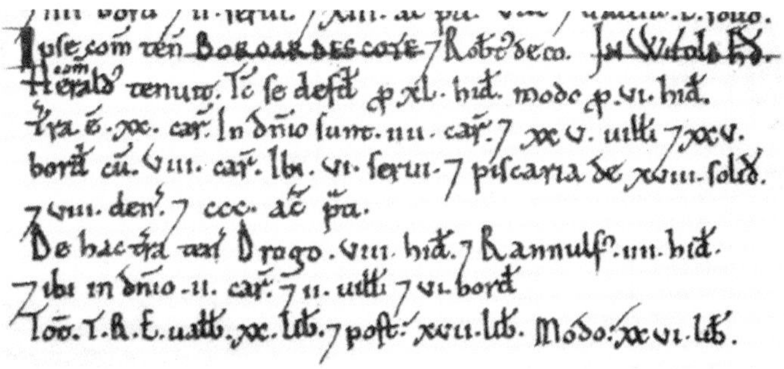

'Boroardescote' in the Domesday Book

The parish church of St Mary the Virgin stands close to the southern bank of the Thames, after the river has passed Lechlade and where it begins its meanderings to the east. The church is not mentioned in the Domesday Book entry but the building dates back in parts to the 13th century and perhaps even earlier.

The medieval village of 'Buscott', which lay to the south of the church, had been abandoned by the 17th century, possibly so that the land could be cleared and used for sheep, as happened in the neighbouring parish of Eaton Hastings. Meanwhile, the manor of Buscot had evolved into three estates: Michael's Court, Paynell's Court and Philip's Court. The Loveden family acquired the Michael's Court estate from Sir Francis Stonor in 1557.

Edward and his first wife Margaret were among the principal benefactors of the church in the late 18th century. They paid for a communion cup and plate to be gilded and donated a silver gilt paten and flagon, in 1779, the same year that saw several family bereavements. In 1788 the right of appointing a clergyman to the church benefice became vested in Edward alone, after he purchased Philip's (or Philpot's) Court from the Throckmortons and amalgamated it with Michael's Court.

St Mary the Virgin, the parish church of Buscot
by Ruth Gerring, 2014

The church contains a number of prominent memorials to the Lovedens and their ancestors. On the north wall of the nave there is one commemorating Edward's great-grandparents Edward and Martha Loveden and five of their children, who predeceased their father:

To the Pious Memory of
The best of Husbands, Fathers, & of Friends
EDWARD LOVEDEN Esq;
Who dyed the 12th day of May 1713
And his Children
EDWARD,RICHARD,LETICE,SUSANNA,&KATHARINE
All whose Bodyes lye Inter'd near this Place
This monument was Erected by
His Widdow and their Mother
Mrs MARTHA LOVEDEN of this Parish
Anno Domini 1717.
MRS MARTHA LOVEDEN
Died the 15th of March 1736

There is a similar marble plaque to the memory of Edward's parents, Thomas Townsend and his wife, Jane, and their son Robert Baker Townsend:

To the Memory of
THOMAS TOWNSEND of Cirencester in the
County of Gloucester, Gent.
JANE his Wife and ROBERT
BAKER TOWNSEND their Son:

JANE TOWNSEND	}		{ 10th March 1757 }		{ 31 }	
THOMAS TOWNSEND	}	died	{ 1st January 1767 }	aged	{ 44 }	Yrs
ROBERT BAKER TOWNSEND	}		{ 11th January 1776 }		{ 21 }	

The death of Edward's first wife Margaret is marked by an elaborate plaque on the north wall in the chancel, recording his love for her and her many qualities:

This Monument
was erected by
EDWARD LOVEDEN LOVEDEN Esqr
to perpetuate the Memory
of MARGARET his beloved Wife
who was the only Daughter, and sole Heiress
of LEWIS PRYSE Esqr (by MARGARET his Wife)
late of New Woodstock, in the County of Oxford,
and Gogerthan, in the County of Cardigan, South Wales.

She was a Lady of exemplary Piety,
and elegant Accomplishments:
adorned with the sweetest Disposition,
and most gentle Manners.
Charitable without Ostentation,
and, in the Discharge of her several Duties,
to her Parents, Husband, Children and Friends,
a Pattern worthy of Imitation.

She died at Buscot Park the thirtieth Day of January,
1784, aged 36 Years;
and was interred in a Vault near this Place,
with three of her Children,
who died in their Infancy:
leaving an only Son, PRYSE LOVEDEN
and two Daughters,
MARGARET and JANE,
surviving her.

Detail from the memorial to Margaret Loveden

Weeping cherub with handkerchief

Detail from the memorial to Margaret Loveden

Detail from the memorial to Elizabeth Loveden

Nearby is the plaque memorialising his second wife Elizabeth, which is equally expressive of his loss:

In a Vault near this Place are interr'd the remains of
ELIZABETH, Second Wife of
EDWARD LOVEDEN LOVEDEN Esqr the only surviving Daughter,
And Sole Heiress of JOHN DARKER of Gayton in the County of Northampton Esqr
She died at Buscot Park, the 26th January 1788
In the 35th Year of her Age;

Deservedly regretted by all who happy in her Acquaintance had been Witnesses
To her sincere Friendship, benevolent Humanity, engaging Manners and
Amiable Disposition, uniformly shown through Life. But by none could
She be so much lamented as by him, who caused this Monument to be Erected.
Sacred to the Memory of her Merit and his Affection.

The vaults "near this place" that are referred to in these memorials are probably burial places within the church. Below the bell-tower, for example, there are floor stones bearing other Loveden inscriptions: one commemorates Edward's great-uncle and he, the last male representative of the ancestral Loveden line, also left an annuity to be paid from the Weston property to provide four coats yearly for four poor men of the parish.

~ COATS OF ARMS ~

A number of Loveden-related coats of arms were once discernible among the memorials to be found in the church at Buscot. Today some are partly or wholly obliterated. We are indebted to P. S. Spokes MA for his 1933 publication 'Coats of Arms in Berkshire Churches' for preserving a record of these arms.

The arms of Loveden are shown with those of Pryse and Darker – these being the family names of Edward's first two wives – and 'in pretence', that is combined to indicate marriage.

Loveden

Gules a bend between four sinister hands erect couped argent, and for a crest on a wreath of the colours, a tyger sejeant or, gorged with a ducal coronet argent.

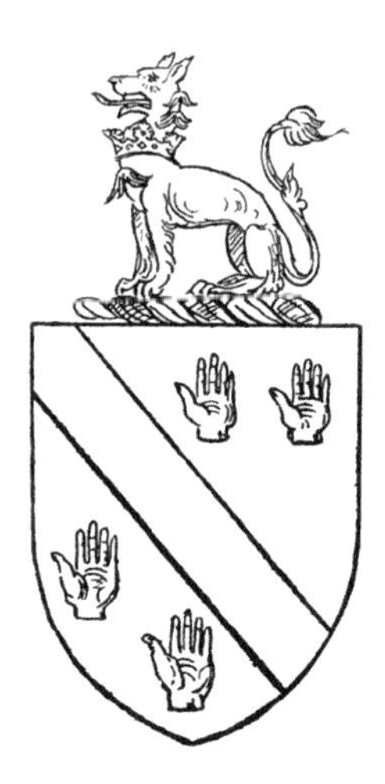

These arms were granted to Edward in 1772.

Pryse

Or a lion rampant reguardant sable.

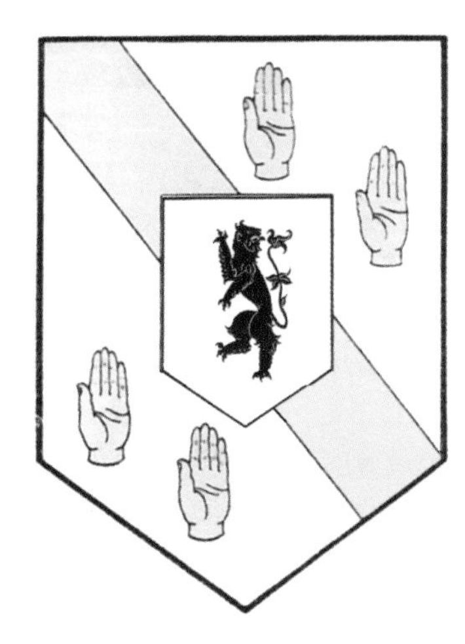

Loveden-Pryse

Darker

Argent on three mounts vert as many hop vines with their poles proper.

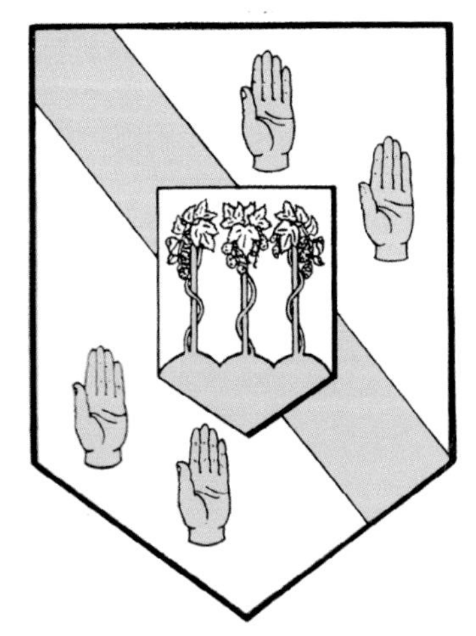

Loveden-Darker

The escutcheon at Weston Farm

A carved stone escutcheon apparently bearing the arms of Loveden, possibly with an inescutcheon, can be seen on a plaque in the wall at Weston Farm house. The whole plaque has been rotated 90° before being set in the wall of the house.

If we show the escutcheon in its correct aspect the 'bend argent' is not present and the central inescutcheon (if that's what it is) is not decipherable.

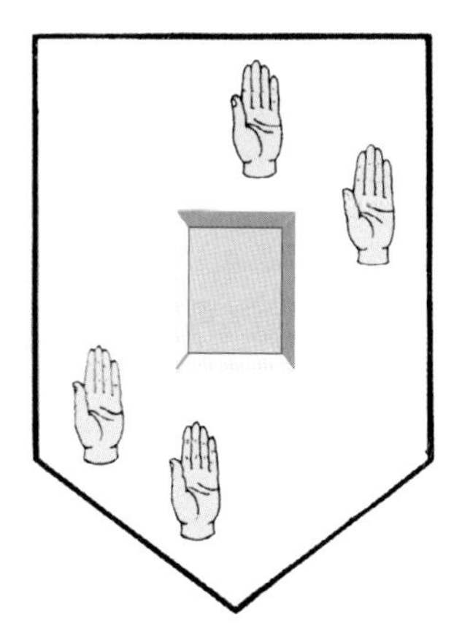

The inscribed lettering "T D" on the escutcheon is probably not significant.

~ LOVEDEN FAMILY TREE 1 ~

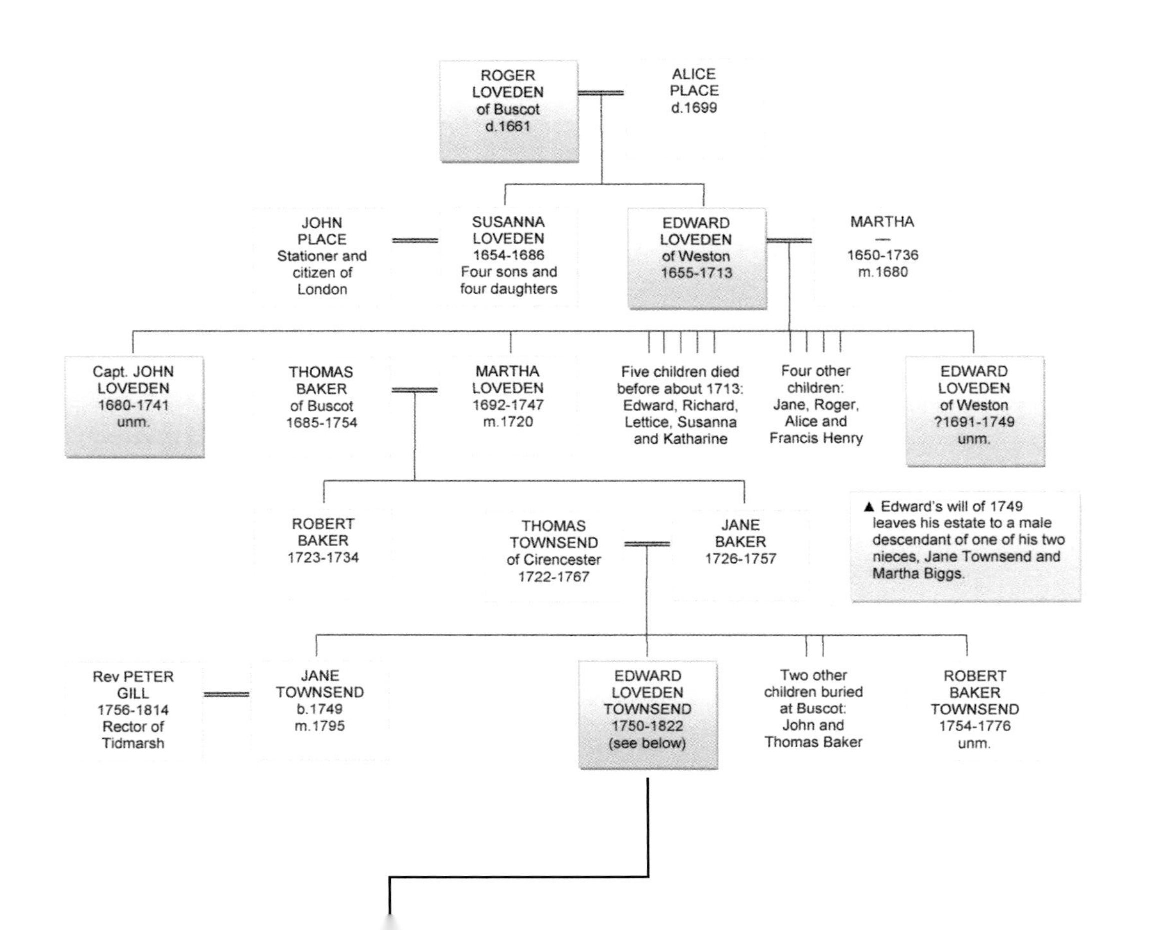

~ LOVEDEN FAMILY TREE 2 ~

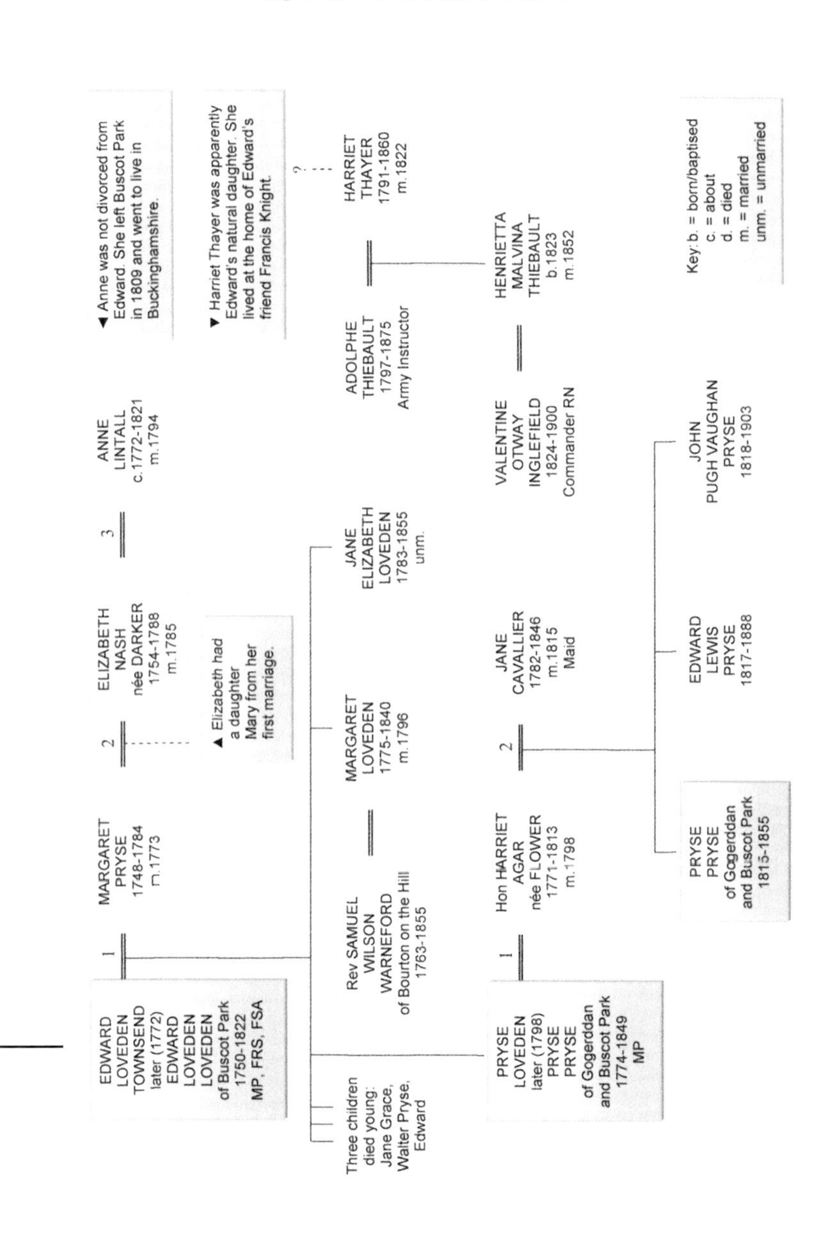

~ SOURCES ~

In researching the material for this booklet, the following items have either been consulted directly or been referred to or quoted from by others. This work also uses material derived from public sector information licensed under the Open Government Licences.

Books

Those book titles marked with an asterisk were accessed online:

A BRIEF HISTORY OF THE PARISH CHURCH OF ST MARY THE VIRGIN BUSCOT (1999) by Ian Beckwith

A TOPOGRAPHICAL MAP OF THE COUNTY OF BERKSHIRE (1761) by J. Rocque

A TOUR THROUGH THE WHOLE ISLAND OF GREAT BRITAIN (1724) by D. Defoe

* ANNALS & ANTIQUITIES OF THE COUNTIES AND COUNTY FAMILIES OF WALES (1872) by Thomas Nicholas

BROKEN LIVES: MARITAL SEPARATION AND DIVORCE IN ENGLAND 1660–1857 (1993) by Lawrence Stone

BUSCOT PARK & THE FARINGDON COLLECTION (2004) published for the Trustees of the Faringdon Collection

BY THAMES, COLN AND LEACH (1927) by William J. Monk

COATS OF ARMS IN BERKSHIRE CHURCHES (1933) by P. S. Spokes, reprinted from The Berkshire Archaeological Journal Vol.37, No.1

ENGLISH SOCIETY IN THE 18TH CENTURY (1990) by Roy Porter

GENERAL VIEW OF THE AGRICULTURE OF BERKSHIRE (1809) by William Mavor

* GENTLEMAN'S MAGAZINE (passim)

* HISTORY OF THE ROYAL BERKSHIRE MILITIA: Now 3rd Battalion Royal Berks Regiment (1897) by Emma Elizabeth Thoyts Cope

IN THE NATURE OF CITIES: URBAN POLITICAL ECOLOGY AND THE POLITICS OF URBAN METABOLISM... (2006) edited by Nikolas Heynen et al.

PRIDE AND PREJUDICE (1813) by Jane Austen

RURAL LIFE IN THE VALE OF THE WHITE HORSE (1974) by Nigel Hammond

THE HISTORICAL AND THE POSTHUMOUS MEMOIRS OF SIR NATHANIEL WRAXALL 1772–1784 (1884) edited by H. B. Wheatley

THE HORSE HOEING HUSBANDRY (1731) by Jethro Tull

THE HOUSE OF COMMONS 1790-1820 (1986) by R. G. Thorne

THE NATURAL HISTORY OF SELBORNE: with observations on various parts of nature and the Naturalist's calendar by Gilbert White (1870) edited by Edward Jesse

THE THAMES & SEVERN CANAL (2009) by Humphrey Household

THE VISITATION OF BERKSHIRE 1664-6 (1882) edited by W. C. MetcalfeFSA

THE WILTS AND BERKS CANAL (2000) by L. J. Dalby

VICTORIA COUNTY HISTORY: BERKSHIRE Vol 4 (1924) edited by William Page and P. H. Ditchfield

Websites

The website addresses of these portals were correct at the time of writing:

www.archiveswales.org.uk

www.berksfhs.org.uk – article by John Gurnett (1999)

www.domesdaymap.co.uk – Prof J Palmer & G Slater, University of Hull

www.familysearch.org

www.indiana.edu

www.historyofparliamentonline.org

www.wessexarch.co.uk/office/wales – picture of Loveden House

discovery.nationalarchives.gov.uk

en.wikipedia.org

gallica.bnf.fr

onlinebooks.library.upenn.edu

socialarchive.iath.virginia.edu

Other Sources

AGRARIAN CHANGE IN THE VALE OF WHITE HORSE 1660-1760 (1984) by Mrs Janie Cottis, PhD thesis at the University of Reading

FARINGDON LIBRARY

GLOUCESTERSHIRE ARCHIVES

HOW DOES THE DEVELOPMENT OF BUSCOT PARK HOUSE OVER THE EIGHTEENTH AND NINETEENTH CENTURIES REFLECT THE ECONOMIC, CULTURAL AND SOCIAL DEVELOPMENT OF THE ENGLISH RULING ELITE? (2007) by Joannah Champion, dissertation at the University of Exeter

MONUMENTAL INSCRIPTIONS: BUSCOT (1994) microfiche by Oxfordshire Family History Society

NATIONAL LIBRARY OF WALES

NATIONAL TRUST: Vernacular Buildings Survey, for Buscot Manor

THE LOVEDEN PAPERS held by Berkshire Record Office

THE NATIONAL ARCHIVES, KEW

WILTS & BERKS CANAL TRUST schematic map (2012) by Doug Small

~ NOTES ~

- The dates associated with the life events of people mentioned, both in the text and in the family tree, are not always consistent in the printed and online sources and are in some cases only guessable. We have used the most commonly accepted dates and guesses. We would welcome any evidence that would allow corrections or additions to be made.

- Where amounts in pounds (or guineas) are quoted we would like to have supplied the present-day equivalents; unfortunately such conversions are not an exact science and authorities differ in their calculations. If you multiply figures in the text by 100 it will give you some idea of Edward's economic standing in today's money.

- The Whigs constituted a political faction that opposed absolute rule and favoured a constitutional monarchy, with the backing of prominent, landed families. Unlike the Tories they supported economic protectionism rather than free trade. In the 19th century they formed the basis of what became the Liberal party.

- The Domesday entry for Buscot refers to "twenty ploughlands" and the ploughland is a measure of land based on the area that a team of eight oxen can plough in a year. This can vary according to the type of soil, of course, but we have assumed 1 ploughland = 120 acres.

- For your own notes...